"An indispensable guide for making your company better and a useful part of any business process improvement toolkit."

David Siegel, fmr. Chairman & CEO, Avis-Budget Group; fmr. Pres & CEO, US Airways

"*Feedback Rules!* offers great tips and helpful ideas for retailers that want to listen more attentively to their customers and employees."

Peter Larkin, President and CEO, National Grocers Association (NGA)

"Nonprofit organizations are always looking for effective ways to listen to their constituents. *Feedback Rules!* provides many useful ideas whether you are a small nonprofit or a large institution."

Quenton Marty, President, Matter

"*Feedback Rules!* provides easy-to-understand tips you can put to use immediately, whether you have extensive experience or are working on your very first project! Listening effectively to our clients is core to our work at Kairos. This book is a must-read for all of our consultants. Highly recommended!"

Jeff Kjellberg, Principal Owner, Kairos & Associates

"There's often a big gap between what a marketer thinks customers want and what customers really want. *Feedback Rules!* provides a comprehensive guide of how to plan and execute feedback programs to help you close that gap."

Lonny Kocina, CEO, Media Relations

D0907403

"A simple yet comprehensive view of how to convert feedback into business results. Invaluable to any organization."

James G. Conroy, President and CEO, Boot Barn

"Keep *Feedback Rules!* in the top drawer of your desk ... a must-have reference guide for sustaining optimal customer satisfaction!"

Sean Novick, Senior Vice President, Northeast Great Dane

"Feedback is the breakfast of champions. Doug and Brian are the gourmet chefs who help you eat right."

Judd Hoekstra, Vice President, Central Region, The Ken Blanchard Companies

"*Feedback Rules!* is a fresh and entertaining reminder of the importance of making feedback an essential part of any corporate culture, and it provides a fantastic framework for ensuring that your company's feedback process is truly best-in-class."

Mark J. Censoprano, Chief Marketing Officer, Aspen Dental Management, Inc.

"Brian and Doug distill their wealth of knowledge on research and feedback down to highly usable nuggets of wisdom in this book."

Bill Bishop, Chief Architect, Brick Meets Click

"In an era when social media has forever changed the customer experience game, *Feedback Rules!* is an invaluable resource for business owners, and those who heed its practical wisdom and guidance should expect to see results. I strongly recommend it to anyone interested in harnessing the power of feedback to enhance the customer experience of their business while further capitalizing on opportunities to extend its reach."

Meg Major, Chief Content Editor, Progressive Grocer

FEEDBACK Rules!

FEEDBACK Rules!

52 ways to listen to your stakeholders

by **DOUG MADENBERG**
and **BRIAN NUMAINVILLE**

illustrated by
STEVE HICKNER

BRIGANTINE MEDIA

Illustrations by Steve Hickner

Brigantine Media
211 North Avenue, St. Johnsbury, Vermont 05819
Phone: 802-751-8802 | Fax: 802-751-8804
E-mail: neil@brigantinemedia.com
Website: www.brigantinemedia.com

ISBN 978-1-9384065-2-2

Doug's Dedication

In the spirit of focusing on the basic rules that really matter, I simply share my gratitude for Jill, Amanda, Eric, and our family. Nothing matters more.

Brian's Dedication

For Maja, thank you for all of your support throughout the twists and turns of life. It means the world to me! And for Josh and Joe, you make your father proud each and every day!

Joint Dedication

We dedicate this book to our fathers, Joe Madenberg and Woody Numainville, in whose footsteps we proudly follow. And a special thank you to Harold Lloyd, our friend and mentor.

The Rules

The Rules

ORGANIZATIONS WOULD NOT exist without stakeholders—employees, customers, members, service recipients, business partners, and the like. Feedback from these constituents provides critical information. What are their needs and how well are you meeting them? How is your company or organization perceived internally and externally? How satisfied is a customer with a product you provide, or with a store visit or service experience? By listening and responding to your stakeholders, you achieve your goals more efficiently and effectively.

This book contains fifty-two rules to help you plan your program, execute it, and respond to stakeholder feedback. These rules come from the experience of the authors over the more than twenty years they have each been designing feedback and research programs for businesses and nonprofit organizations.

The book is divided into three sections. The rules in the first section, Ground Rules, pertain to the planning and setup of an effective survey or feedback program. Review these rules completely, as they constitute the building blocks of a solid foundation that must be in place before moving ahead.

Part two, Rules of Engagement, offer advice on the specifics of your feedback process. From choosing the audience to planning the content, these rules cover how to design your program so it will provide valid and useful information.

Of utmost importance are the Golden Rules in

part three. These are rules to help you make sense of the results of your feedback program. We recommend ways to communicate the results to your stakeholders and offer techniques for responding to feedback effectively.

It's exciting to embark on a program to get feedback from your stakeholders. We hope you find *Feedback Rules!* to be a practical and useful guide through the process.

PART ONE

Ground Rules

Make sure you're ready.

YOUR COMPANY MANAGEMENT is considering a feedback program. How do you decide if the time is right? Assess whether or not the organization is ready.

Do these exist?

- A realistic budget
- The willingness to objectively accept the findings (good and bad)
- Buy-in across the organization
- The fortitude to make changes based on the results

Carefully consider these prerequisites. If the organization is eager on all fronts but has no budget for the research, the time isn't right. If the money is available but upper management isn't willing to accept the findings and make changes, don't spend the money, because nothing will result from the effort.

If you can answer "yes" to all four questions in the readiness test—ready, get set, and ... go!

Be in it for the long term.

A FEEDBACK PROGRAM is a long-term investment, not the "flavor of the month." Use the feedback program to show that you care about experiences on an ongoing basis.

A customer feedback program is a vehicle to tell you what you are doing right and where you need to improve. But it's also a way to show customers that you care about them. When the door is open for customers to tell you about their experiences, it magnifies the value of the program.

We had one past client who really did care about their customers' experiences. But when it came to implementing and using a feedback program, the commitment wasn't strong enough to stick with it. The store managers were not given access to the system for about a year, and the responses were handled by a part-time employee who would deal with only the most burning issues. This created a situation that didn't benefit the customers or the organization. In the end, the company wasn't really in it for the long term and stopped using the feedback program.

Feedback programs are long-term investments. The value comes from offering an ongoing dialogue about experiences with your organization.

Who's your customer?

MY CUSTOMER? THAT'S easy—it's the person who shops at my store or buys a service my company offers.

Well, that's not always the right answer. Everyone has a customer. Your customer might be an internal one, such as another department that you support at work. Your customer might not be a paying one, such as a recipient in need of a meal from a nonprofit.

No matter who your customer is, listening to customers' needs is vital.

Employees within an organization sometimes lack a connection to the external consumer of their products or services. This is where focusing on the internal customers, such as other departments or locations, provides a basis for measuring and responding to feedback.

Whether internal or external, everyone has a customer and feedback is important. Listening and responding to customers show that we care about their needs and helps build loyalty.

Interview your business partners.

FEEDBACK PROGRAMS AREN'T just to hear from customers or employees. Sometimes organizations need to assess their relationships with other companies with whom they work. This can be important feedback, but collecting it can present unique challenges.

We work with companies where consumers are not the only "customer." There are retail sales channels, distribution subsidiaries, and other stakeholders who interact on a daily basis with the organization. People in these positions can all add valuable insight.

The best way to get feedback from business partners is through in-depth phone interviews. You'll usually get a strong response rate to such interviews, since it's harder to ignore a real interviewer on the phone than a survey sent via e-mail.

These interviews must be conducted by experienced interviewers who are comfortable dealing with business professionals. You'll have to schedule the interviews in order to reach the target audience.

Handle business partner feedback programs carefully so that you receive high-quality information that can help improve your business and keep your partner relationship strong.

Get social media feedback.

PUBLIC COMMENTS ON social media provide another avenue to listen and converse with your stakeholders.

If you are a large organization there will likely be chatter about you in social media. A smaller company should create its own channel on Facebook, Twitter, or other social media to solicit feedback and listen. And don't limit yourself to your own channel—check out what your competitors are doing and what people are saying about them on social media. If you want to hear employees talking about your company, a

platform like Glassdoor gives employees the ability to sound off about what it's really like to work there.

Today, organizations are expected to engage with stakeholders immediately, and social media channels give you direct access.

Wink, a home automation company, experienced a problem with many hubs locking up and no longer functioning. Wink immediately started communicating with affected individuals, not just by e-mail, but also through interactive communication on social media. The company was particularly active on Twitter, using the channel to repeatedly apologize and try to help. Brian was personally impacted by this outage and utilized Twitter to converse with the company. He was pleasantly surprised at how quickly they responded to his feedback despite what must have been chaos at the company!

Caveat: One limitation of listening to social media is that it may not be representative of the broadest base of your stakeholders, so be careful when generalizing from this source. But in combination with other feedback tools, valuable information is available from social media.

Make your case.

ONCE YOU HAVE decided to implement a feedback program, you need to sell it to the organization. You need strong support from the top, and you might have to convince the C-suite why a feedback program is important and how it can help transform your organization.

What if we never listened to our stakeholders? We would miss tremendous opportunities to improve our organization to better serve those who we exist to help or to whom we provide our product or service. We would operate in a vacuum, built on our own perceptions of how well we are doing as an organization.

Feargal Quinn, when he was the owner of Superquinn Markets in Ireland, initiated a customer focus group program to get feedback directly from

small groups of customers. But Quinn went one step further. As he greeted the customers when they arrived for the focus group, he told them, "Don't give me any positive feedback. I don't need you to tell me what we're doing well. I want to hear what you don't like and where we're not meeting your expectations." Quinn knew it was easy to hear the good feedback, but that wasn't the information that would help them improve. (PS: Superquinn was generally recognized as one of the top supermarkets in the world when Quinn was at the helm.)

Listening to the voice of the customer (whether internal or external) through a feedback program allows us to know where we stand and what we can do better, based on information from those using our products or services, or working for us, rather than our own internal perceptions. In short, we become customer-centric in our approach!

Make the case for a feedback program in your organization. You'll gain valuable perspective by listening to customers and learn how to serve them better.

Take baby steps.

A FEEDBACK PROGRAM might seem like a monumental task. It takes a lot of time, money, and effort to put a good program together and make it valuable.

Start with baby steps! Run a small pilot program first to see how it works and make whatever adjustments might be needed before rolling it out.

In a pilot research project you can test out a survey on a small number of people to determine if all the questions are clear. You can implement a pilot program in a few locations before finalizing the survey topics or the method of data collection, and then roll it out to your whole organization.

A Fortune 500 conglomerate used a mystery shopper program for many years. When the company was ready to implement a trip-specific feedback program that surveyed actual customers, it started with a pilot program in a few stores to evaluate its effectiveness. As a result of the pilot, they determined that using a combination of a phone-based and web-based approach garnered the most shopper responses. The program was then rolled out in all the corporate-owned stores, ultimately replacing the mystery shopper program.

Starting with a pilot program provides an easy way to evaluate not only the program's effectiveness, but also helps you understand how it works so you can iron out field communication and reporting.

Tune in to the best channel.

THERE ARE MANY ways to gather feedback. How do you choose the best feedback channel for your company?

Should I use an automated feedback program? Focus groups? Would a web survey be better? What about a social media poll? Can I use more than one method?

The best channel depends on your goal for the feedback. Here are some alternatives:

- Automated Feedback Program—automatically invites the customer to give feedback (for example, printed on a register receipt). This works best when you want to get an ongoing pulse on your organization and when hear from as many constituents as possible. The best automated feedback programs provide multiple ways for feedback to be collected, including interactive voice response (IVR) and web.

- Focus Group—works well when you are trying to dig deep to explore reactions to something, such as advertising, or when an in-depth discussion of a topic is appropriate. A focus group typically involves only a small number of people. Be careful about generalizing the results.

- Web Survey—can be programmed easily, edited quickly, and directly linked into many reporting platforms. This tool is often desired for its cost effectiveness and flexibility.

- Social Media Poll—using social media to conduct a poll, such as on a Facebook page, is an inexpensive way to collect feedback. This type of poll provides a vehicle that is accessible to a generation of consumers that are plugged into social media.

Sometimes combining two or more methods of feedback will provide the best results.

Suppose you are planning to put together focus groups about the shopping experience at a particular retail store but are not sure about what issues shoppers might be encountering during their store visits. Start by reviewing the results of an automated feedback program to look at the high and low scoring departments and services. That will help you determine what areas to emphasize in your focus groups.

Choosing the right channel for listening to customers helps you "tune in" to the feedback you need.

Stay inside or go outside.

ESTABLISHING AND RUNNING a feedback program requires specific skills. Should you have someone within your organization build the feedback program or go outside to a professional?

If you have someone in your organization with real expertise on feedback programs, that may be the way to go. That person can use one of the many "do it yourself" tools to create your survey. But survey questions are both an art and a science, and if you don't have the expertise internally, you'll be better served to use a feedback professional to help get the program up and running, as well as support you through the process.

Make sure outside resources who help with your feedback program know your industry and your organization, are credible and professional, and have the right skills. Even if an internal resource has the skills and ability to build the program, you might want to bring in an outside professional to help you select a tool and provide expertise and learning from other programs they have implemented.

The needed skills to build an effective feedback program may be available inside your organization or you may need to leverage outside expertise. The time and effort spent up front ensuring your program is soundly constructed will be well worth it down the road.

Use web and phone for feedback.

SURVEYS CAN BE conducted either online or by telephone. Each tool offers different strengths and weaknesses. Don't choose—use both. The key is to provide options to increase respondent participation.

Web surveys work great among those comfortable with using computers, mobile devices, and smartphones. However, they don't work well if the respondent is not comfortable with digital devices or is hesitant to answer questions online about certain topics, such as providing personal information.

Phone surveys, including inbound Interactive Voice Response (IVR) for feedback, work better when the respondent is more comfortable using a phone, or if the topic requires probing for more depth.

Many times an organization may choose to use a web-only feedback platform because it is less expensive and "everyone is using the Internet nowadays." Unfortunately, this simply isn't true, and important feedback will be missed by going this route.

In our experience, the best feedback programs include both a web and phone option. Respondents can choose between the options, and the participation rate will be higher when they decide how to engage with your organization. Sometimes respondents choose an option based on personal preference; other times the choice may be situational, based on where they are when they want to provide the feedback.

The easier you make it for respondents to give feedback, the better the results of your program will be.

Flow feedback together.

ORGANIZATIONS RECEIVE FEEDBACK from a wide variety of vehicles, including customer feedback programs, social media, website "contact us" forms, and call centers. How do you make sure that all of this data comes together so it can be used?

Integrate all the inputs into a common reporting platform that allows the appropriate people in the organization to review and respond to the feedback.

Many of our clients tie their feedback vehicles together. Store managers receive feedback from different inputs on a daily basis, which allows them

to respond quickly and eliminates the need for a "gatekeeper" to manually route feedback to the correct party.

Flow your feedback vehicles together to streamline the process and ensure that feedback reaches those who need to take action as quickly as possible.

Timing is everything.

DETERMINING HOW OFTEN to run a feedback program should be based on how the information will be used. An ongoing program makes sense if you have the opportunity to act on the information very quickly. If it will take time to implement changes, finish your program first, then act on it before your start a new round of surveys.

If you are collecting feedback at store visits, the program can continue on an ongoing basis. You'll want to make fast changes based on customer input. However, employee or business partner surveys lend themselves to much less frequent intervals so you have time to make changes before the next survey is conducted.

We work with supermarkets that collect thousands of surveys from shoppers each month. Many store managers on our program rely heavily on this information to stay in touch with shopper concerns.

Collecting and responding to the feedback quickly is important to their operations. In this case, an ongoing frequency is the right interval. One store manager of a supermarket client observed, "A customer may have a bad experience. If you didn't get a chance to talk about it with that person, you might lose that customer. The survey mechanism allows the customer to have an opportunity to vent. Often, they are quite impressed when you call back or resolve their issue. It can save a relationship."

Carefully consider how often you run your feedback programs. Set the frequency of collecting feedback based on your ability to respond or make appropriate changes.

Plan the process.

AT THE SAME time your feedback program is being developed, you have to plan for the next steps that will come after the results are in. Plan how your organization will take the information from the program and turn it into action.

Think about how you will evaluate your progress. If data is collected on an ongoing basis, the planning will focus more on regularly evaluating progress made on key metrics—comparing quarter-to-quarter, for example. If your feedback is taken at set intervals— such as an annual employee survey—a year-over-year comparison makes more sense.

Beyond measuring progress, you also need to develop action plans to address areas of opportunity.

You can use a top-down approach and have management develop directives, or a bottom-up approach where employee teams identify and implement actions to improve performance.

A feedback program that is well planned from the start has the best chance for success in any organization.

Designate an owner.

FEEDBACK NEEDS AN "owner" in every organization. Without a designated home, the feedback may end up in a report that no one reads.

Larger organizations may have a dedicated department or staff person who takes charge of the feedback. Often the marketing department or operations takes the lead with feedback programs. This usually provides a good fit, since these departments are focused on and close to the customer. If the feedback is about employees, the human resources department is probably the best home for the information.

Smaller organizations have to decide who owns their feedback. The key is making sure that a person or group has the interest and authority to act on the information that's uncovered.

Remember, the people who are providing feedback, whether internal or external, are doing so with the hope that their voices will be heard and acted upon. By having a designated owner, this valuable input won't be lost.

Neutralize the naysayers.

NOT EVERYONE EMBRACES feedback initiatives. Whether it's self-preservation by an underperforming manager, unwillingness by an executive who's too tired to make needed changes, or power trips by associates who try to influence others negatively, there are always naysayers when a feedback program is being implemented.

You'll have to neutralize those naysayers if you want your feedback program to succeed.

Consider Mary, a long-term employee at a company that's been in business for more than 100 years. Over the last several decades (as long as Mary has worked there), the company has seen many changes in management. Each time a new CEO has come in, there has been another round of employee surveys. In

Mary's mind, those surveys were just to weed out people who wouldn't fit in. She has always felt that despite all the surveys, nothing seems to change for the better. So when the new CEO arrived, sure enough, another employee survey followed. Jenny, a new employee, expressed excitement at being able to share her opinion. Mary told her not to bother, that it wouldn't make any difference. Jenny began to wonder if she had made the right choice to join this organization.

How do you handle the Marys in your organization? Communication!

- Explain to employees how you are making sure the feedback captures input from as many people as possible.

- Tell employees that the feedback will serve as a representative basis for understanding issues.

- Make it clear that the goal is to listen to stakeholders and use that information to improve.

- Stress that the feedback will not be used to punish anyone.

- Make sure that the results and their corresponding action plans are openly communicated throughout the organization.

Naysayers can kill a feedback program. Neutralize them before you start!

Out with the old, in with the new.

WHEN YOU LAUNCH a new feedback program, make sure that any tools used in the past to get customer feedback are retired.

Check for old comment card programs, customer feedback hotlines, and other types of feedback tools. These can be confusing if they are still available when a new program is launched. Customers won't know which one to use, and you'll jeopardize the effectiveness of the new program.

When we launch a new program, we do an in-store audit, walking through the client's stores to look for these forgotten tools. Before the new program begins, we get rid of all vestiges of old feedback tools that we find.

You'd be surprised how often a store still has old suggestion cards near the checkout stands or a "How are we doing?" phone number still printed on the cash register receipt. Make sure those old programs are laid to rest so the new program has a fair chance to collect accurate information.

Launch with enthusiasm!

LAUNCHING A STAKEHOLDER feedback initiative takes a great deal of preparation and planning. Once the time is right, launch the program with enthusiasm!

Start by creating internal excitement about the program. Make the launch fun and exciting for your employees. Consider running contests between departments and showcasing the results internally.

Don't make it feel like the program is just more work. Let employees know the program will help them serve customers better by listening to them and responding to their needs more effectively.

One retailer that we worked with really wanted to make sure its feedback program launched the right way. The management team was fully committed to the program, and that enthusiasm cascaded down to employees. The company went all out with bag stuffers and store signage to make sure that shoppers were aware of the program. When the program was up and running, they regularly recognized the shoppers who won the ongoing sweepstakes incentive.

An enthusiastic launch to a new stakeholder feedback program pays big dividends, because everyone benefits.

Promote, promote, promote.

EVERYONE'S BUSY. IT'S easy to forget about that survey you were asked to take the other day. What's a company that's looking for feedback to do?

Keep promoting the program from its launch until the end date.

Consider all your communication vehicles that will reach the target audience—then use them. Newsletters, direct mail, websites, apps, and even face-to-face encounters with salespeople or customer reps are all ways your company can communicate with the people you want to reach. Give the highest priority to the vehicles that most directly and

regularly expose the program to your target audience. Evaluate which methods work best throughout the duration of the program and use the most successful ones more frequently. A short-term survey will probably lend itself to different communication tools than an ongoing, long-term feedback program.

Promote your feedback program as long as it is underway. That's the best approach for getting strong participation and useful feedback.

PART TWO

Rules of Engagement

Determine your target.

HOW DO YOU decide whether to solicit feedback from everyone or just survey a sample?

Including the entire population means everyone has the opportunity to be heard. But it may be far more cost-effective to select a sample.

The size of the potential population is one way to make the decision. If the size of the group to be surveyed is small, it may be easy to ask for (and even collect) feedback from nearly everyone. The method used to collect the information can also help determine whether to survey the whole population or a sample. For example, if your program prints an invitation to participate in the survey on a register receipt, you will be inviting everyone in your customer base to take part.

Other situations call for asking for feedback from only a sample of the whole population. For example, if you want to conduct an in-depth survey about a specific retail location, it is impossible to interview everyone who visits the store. A sample of visitors must suffice. Careful thought must be given to make sure the sample is representative of the broader population being studied.

So, everyone or just some people? It depends on the size of your group, how you're collecting the data, and what's feasible.

Keep it confidential.

PEOPLE ARE CONCERNED about maintaining their privacy and the security of their personal information. When you ask for feedback, your audience needs to know that their personal information will be kept confidential.

There are many considerations. If you ask for a respondent's name and contact information, it must be opt-in. Ask and then respect whether the respondent wants further contact from you. Clearly communicate how the information will be used.

When you are conducting an employee survey, participants may not want to be identified, especially if they point out problems or concerns. Assure respondents that any personal information, such as an employee ID number, is only being used to confirm that the survey is valid and has come from a current employee. Using an outside research service provides additional reassurance to many employees that their individual comments will not be made available to their managers.

Often, management is concerned that employees will be unwilling to include their employee number when filling out a survey. Our experience suggests that this issue can be addressed with honest communication. Let employees know that their employee number is only to ensure that the responses are valid. When companies explain it to employees, typically only a few people will refuse to participate.

Keep your respondents' personal information confidential, and let them know that's what you're doing.

Make it worthwhile.

THE CARROT OR the stick? Use the carrot for your feedback program. Providing an incentive to participate will help get more respondents for your ongoing feedback program.

People don't *have* to respond to your survey—they *choose* to. Make it worth their while to expend the effort. An incentive, such as a sweepstakes or a coupon for money off on their next shopping trip, is often just the ticket for encouraging participation in the feedback program.

There is another reason why incentives are smart. An incentive encourages a broad range of participants to provide their input. Without one, you are likely to only hear from very upset or very satisfied customers

. . . but not the multitudes in between. When that happens, the results you get from the feedback don't really represent all your stakeholders.

Make it worthwhile to participate in your feedback program. It's money well spent to make sure your feedback is worthwhile, too.

Ask for permission.

CERTAIN USES OF feedback require permission. If you plan to use the feedback in a way that attaches the identity of the feedback to an individual in a public fashion, you must get permission before using it.

Your program may include a once-a-month prize drawing from all the people who participated in the feedback program each month. If you plan to showcase those winners publicly, you must receive permission to do so. When you take the winner's photograph to publicize it on your website, get her permission in writing.

You might decide to use quotes from some of the feedback respondents in your upcoming advertising.

Again, you'll need to get their permission in writing.

Include a question in the feedback program asking whether or not the respondent will allow you to contact him about his feedback. If the answer is no, this must always be respected. You can get in touch with the people who say "yes," but they will still need to give their written permission for specific use of their names, comments, or photographs.

Most of your customers or employees will be happy to be part of a public campaign—but ask first!

Include only what you can act on.

IN A COURTROOM, never ask a question if you don't already know the answer. In collecting feedback, never ask a question if you can't change the situation afterward. This applies to feedback from employees, customers, or anyone else.

Let's say that you are constructing a survey about a retail store. The store has a tight parking lot but there is nothing that can be done to improve the situation. The survey includes a question asking customers to rate the parking lot, and then asks for suggestions about the parking lot. So a number of

customers respond that the parking lot is too tight, and suggest that the store build a garage over the retail store to park cars.

This question should have never been asked. The store can't enlarge its lot and could never afford to construct a garage above the store's building. By asking the question about the parking lot, the retailer has done nothing but remind the respondent of a problem that can't be fixed.

Companies mistakenly include questions about compensation when surveying employees. But it is unlikely that the organization will makes changes to its compensation structure based on input from employees. Don't ask that kind of question unless you are actually willing to consider the feedback seriously.

As you consider collecting feedback, carefully evaluate every question. If a question is about something you cannot or will not change, don't ask it!

Respect people's time.

SURVEYS SEEM TO pop up everywhere today! Whether we are visiting a restaurant, shopping online, flying on a plane, or having our car serviced, companies ask customers to provide feedback on the experience. You don't want your customers to think, "another questionnaire to answer . . ." Be aware of how often everyone is asked to give feedback and respect people's time as you construct your surveys.

Make a survey too long and your completion rate will certainly drop. On the other hand, if you make it too short you could miss valuable input. How do you decide what to keep in and what to leave out?

First, separate the "need to know" from the "nice to know" when building the survey. There is a tendency to include every possible question in a survey rather than focus on specifically what is needed. Resist this urge.

Second, once you have the questions together that you think need to be included, time the survey. If it feels too long to you, it is!

Finally, evaluate opportunities to use more precise and targeted surveys. For example, when testing a new program in a store, don't add it to the broader customer satisfaction survey. Find a way to conduct a targeted survey focusing on the shoppers who are visiting that particular department.

One way to respect people's time is by providing a streamlined survey for those taking it on a mobile device. A long survey on a smartphone is cumbersome and respondents often give up. If you focus on the key items of importance and ask just those questions, you will improve your response rate while respecting the time of the person filling it out.

People are starved for time today. Conduct surveys that are the right length and capture just the information you really need to know.

Speak the right language.

TO CLEARLY COMMUNICATE with the target audience of a feedback program, adopt the commonly used language for the industry.

Using the right "voice" in a feedback program isn't difficult, but it does require some investigation, especially if you are new to an industry. There are many ways to learn common conventions, such as reading trade publications, conducting interviews with people in the industry, and listening carefully to terms used in conversation.

For example, in the nonprofit sector, certain terminology is more commonly used. Referring to "constituents" rather than "customers" or using the term "fundraising" instead of "sales" are simple but important differences.

Just as you need to speak a country's language to be understood there, you need to clearly communicate using industry terms in your feedback program. If you fail to "speak the right language" you will lower the response rate, jeopardize the accuracy of the information collected, and frustrate respondents.

Construct questions carefully.

GARBAGE IN, GARBAGE out! You can't get useful results from a feedback program unless your questions are constructed the right way. Survey questions need to be objective and unbiased. Be sure the questions don't lead the respondent down any particular path. Most importantly, they must be the right questions to answer what the research is trying to discover.

Start by establishing a cross-functional team to brainstorm all the topics that need to be captured in the survey. Then involve someone with relevant research experience to design the questionnaire. This

researching expert, either an internal or external resource, will manage the survey's length and make sure the questions used do not incorporate any bias or leading language.

Survey questions must have consistency in their construction to avoid confusion and flawed results. Here's an example: consider the following set of statements in a survey. Employees are asked whether they agree or disagree.

- We practice teamwork in our department in order to achieve our goals.

- My supervisor keeps me informed about important issues.

- My supervisors can be overly critical of my work.

The first two are positively worded statements, but statement number three is constructed in a negative way. Agreement with this statement is actually a "bad" thing, and a high score would be a weak result. A careful survey development process would identify this issue before the survey is used and lead to a revision of statement three so that it is worded consistently with the others.

You don't want to waste a lot of time and money on findings that are questionable because the survey was constructed poorly. Create a strong foundation of well-crafted survey questions.

Don't make it too simple.

WOULDN'T IT BE great if there were one "magic question" you could ask to provide all the information you really need to know? Unfortunately, it's not usually that simple. In your zeal to make sure respondents aren't spending too much time giving feedback, be careful that you haven't eliminated questions that you need to get to the heart of the matter.

A questionnaire can become oversimplified. If that happens, it doesn't provide enough useful information.

For example, surveys sometimes only ask about the likelihood to recommend an organization. While this provides valuable information as part of a broader survey, asked alone it doesn't provide any insight about satisfaction, performance, or opportunities for improvement. You don't know why a customer would or would not recommend your company, and those details are crucial to understanding the respondents' answers.

We sometimes see a survey where the choices are all "yes" or "no." Although the person taking the survey may find it easy to complete, this simple approach will result in many missed insights. Include some other question types, such as ratings or open-ended answers, to gather enough detail to be really informative.

Simple is not always better. The appropriate number and right type of questions can yield great rewards.

Use the best scale.

HAVE YOU EVER taken a survey and wondered how somebody came up with the scale used? Why did they use four points or ten points? What is the difference between a five and a six on an eight-point scale?

Find a way to collect data from respondents that makes sense for them and for you. Too often numerical scales are included in surveys with little thought to how respondents will interpret them, resulting in less-than-accurate ratings and hard-to-understand findings.

Think about a numerical scale as if you are the person taking the survey. Typically, a shorter numerical scale is easier for respondents to use accurately because the differences between the numbers are easier to discern and more meaningful. Even a ten-point scale may be too wide a span, and a respondent may have trouble meaningfully differentiating between scores that are just one point apart. (What *is* the difference between a six and a seven, really?) But numerical scales are useful when an average score is desired, so surveys often include them.

There are many other ways, beyond simple numerical scales, to ask meaningful questions. A scale with the words "exceeds," "meets," "nearly meets," and "misses" leaves little room for error in how the respondent rates an experience. A scale like this also provides clear, distinct findings for the researcher.

When planning the questions for a feedback program, use the scale that will give your results accuracy in rating as well as in analyzing the findings.

Count all the ratings.

I SAT ACROSS the desk from the manager of an auto dealership after signing a deal for a new car. "You're going to be getting a customer satisfaction survey from the company," said the manager. I said I'd be glad to participate.

"But it's *really* important that you give us a ten," she continued. "Anything else is basically meaningless. They only count the tens."

Unfortunately, this scene plays out in countless companies when they conduct surveys. They think that only the single highest satisfaction or loyalty rating matters and this "top box score" is what drives the company's performance.

But this approach ignores the richness of

stakeholder feedback and the opportunities to learn from the results. There is knowledge to be gained from every survey response.

Satisfaction and loyalty are not all-or-nothing concepts. When a customer gives a rating of 4 out of 5, that feedback should not simply be discarded. On a ten-point satisfaction scale, a 6 is not the same as a 2.

When you use a numeric rating scale, look at all the available response options when considering the results. Tracking "top box" is a worthwhile exercise, especially when the desire is to live up to the highest possible standards. But other metrics that take *all* the ratings into account (such as an average or weighted score) should be tracked, too.

EXTRA TIP

If you are truly interested in a black-and-white result, frame the survey question this way:

Were you completely satisfied with this experience? *(Yes* or *No)*

This aligns the rating and reporting with the question being asked.

Ask for the "why."

USEFUL FEEDBACK IS more than ratings on a scale. To get the most out of your customer or employee feedback, you need to know *why* people respond as they do.

To get to the "why," incorporate open-ended questions as part of the process.

We live in a numbers-driven world. Whether it's metrics on operational performance or ratings on a feedback program, it feels more precise to collect and analyze numerical performance. But numbers can mean different things to different people. For one person, a "4" on a scale of one to ten is close to average. For others, a "4" means lousy. You'll need to dig deeper to uncover the reasons behind the ratings.

Include both rating questions and open-ended comments when gathering feedback. Taken together, they will help you develop the full picture.

Mind the time (frame).

ALLOW ENOUGH TIME for the target audience to participate in your feedback initiative, but not too much time.

An immediate response to a survey invitation is not practical. Let participants select a time when they can provide a thoughtful response and not feel rushed. You'll show respect for your stakeholders' time, and receive more reliable and actionable information from the survey.

Some surveys require a quicker response. Feedback about a specific event, such as a company meeting, a store visit, or a technical support call, should be collected while the experience is still fresh in the respondent's mind. Once several days have passed, the helpful details begin to fade.

Whatever the allotted timeframe for survey completion, it's a good idea to send a reminder about the survey about halfway between the initial invitation and the due date. Give a final reminder, too, about 24 hours before the survey is scheduled to end. (And make sure you remove the people from your reminders if they have already responded.)

There may be times where you have to extend the survey period if you're not getting enough responses. This may call for an extra reminder.

When we were collecting feedback on certain technology used in the food industry by independent retailers, the target audience was difficult to reach. After the initial announcement of the survey and frequent reminders, we used multiple announcements of the survey in a wide array of industry e-news letters, personal contacts, social media, and ongoing solicitation of responses. We also extended the timeframe of the survey. It took all of these efforts to achieve the response rate we needed.

Allowing enough time and reminding potential participants of their opportunity to provide feedback helps foster a strong response rate and results that will add value.

Weed out bad data.

YOU CAN ONLY trust the results of a feedback program if you are confident that the responses are valid. There are steps you can take to weed out abusive activity by unreliable respondents.

Watch for "speeders"—people who fill out a survey too quickly. Some respondents rush through just to be eligible for the response incentive, often with little (or any) thought to how they are answering. To guard against such "speeders," set a minimum time threshold below which the response is removed from the data prior to reporting.

Carefully monitor respondents who click answers without reading the survey question. One way to counteract this problem is to include a question that instructs the survey-taker to answer "3" for that item.

If the respondent fails this test, the survey is removed.

Check for respondents who fill out a survey or feedback form too often, which may expose people who are trying to get the reward for answering the survey. Establish a threshold number of allowable submitted surveys (such as one completed survey in a week) and monitor for survey submissions across IP addresses, phone numbers, and e-mails.

Employees should not take part in customer feedback programs. It isn't that their feedback is less valuable, but it should be collected in designated employee feedback programs to prevent the customer program from becoming a tool to comment negatively on the store or co-workers, or simply trying to win the incentive.

Get out your hoe and weed out the respondents who aren't helping your survey bear useful fruit!

Testing, 1 ... 2 ... 3 ...

YOU'VE DECIDED TO get feedback. Great! You've worked hard to decide what topics are important and what questions you'll ask. Well done! But you're not quite ready to flip the switch. It's time to test the survey content to refine any issues before you roll out the program.

There are several stages of testing. First, bounce all the topics off an internal, cross-departmental team to make sure that all of the needed topics are covered. Next, test the questions with a small internal team to be sure there are no problems with the language used, and that the questions are clear and elicit direct responses. When you feel that the questions are ready to go, pre-test them with a number of real stakeholders (about 20 to 30 people will give you a good representative sample).

Once you are satisfied with the results of testing, the program is ready to go live. But the work is not over. If the feedback program is an ongoing effort, monitor for questions that seem to be confusing or not gleaning the right type of responses. You can adjust the survey language if necessary to improve the quality of your responses. If the survey takes place periodically, closely examine the results when it is finished and make notes for revising it the next time it is administered.

Take the time to test both the topics and the questions before you start your feedback program so you gain the most value from the responses.

PART THREE

Golden Rules

Respond to respondents.

COLLECTING FEEDBACK SHOULD be more than just reviewing numbers and categorizing comments. Remember, your respondents are real people who have taken the time to offer their feedback. The best way to thank them for their input is to respond personally whenever possible.

You can send an e-mail, a letter, or even make a personal phone call to respond. Use your judgment to decide how you should respond to a concern or a positive comment, depending on the size of the issue. You'll set your company apart from all the rest with this kind of personal attention to feedback.

The best feedback programs create a mechanism for documenting the response to the feedback, as well as any steps taken. This ensures that others know about the contact, creates a permanent record of the interaction, and can also be used to track the organization's effectiveness in responding to feedback. Many of our clients have told us about irate shoppers who became delighted customers when their complaints were handled personally and professionally.

Set yourself apart. Find a way to respond personally to feedback you receive. The goodwill you build will be priceless.

Triage your feedback.

IN THE HOSPITAL emergency room, the intake nurse knows how to triage patients so the most critical ones are seen immediately. A sore throat can wait. The doctor must see a patient with a deep wound right away.

Triage your feedback. Develop a way to separate feedback that needs immediate attention from feedback that can be handled in a timely but not urgent fashion.

Customers will use a feedback program to provide input on a wide range of concerns. Think through the range of issues that could arise and set plans in place to act on feedback right away when it's necessary.

Consider a situation where someone is injured or there is an accident in the parking lot. Or a customer becomes ill after eating food from a restaurant. In these instances, you want this feedback to be addressed quickly and resolved.

One way to ensure that attention is given to the high priorities is to incorporate alerts that are send by text or e-mail directly to someone who can take action when more urgent feedback comes in.

Another way to focus on these comments is to routinely screen for key words in the open-ended feedback provided: words such as "illness," "fell," or "sick" are flags to make sure critical issues don't slip through the cracks.

Triage the feedback to be sure that issues of the utmost importance take priority.

Don't get defensive.

When the feedback starts coming in, even the very best companies hear highly negative criticism. This is normal and, more than that, it's expected. But it's not easy to take!

Don't get defensive when the feedback is less than stellar. Remember, the input you are receiving reflects the perception of the individuals providing it. What they are saying is their reality and it may even have required some courage for them to provide the feedback. Consider it a gift, offered with the best of intentions. (See Rule #44 about complaints.)

When publicly discussing negative feedback, remain positive. Everyone will be watching how you set the example. Finding the right phrasing and tone will go a long way. Make sure you also clearly articulate the reality of the situation, as best as you can determine. Negative feedback is often a bit skewed.

In a feedback program we ran for a supermarket client, this comment was received: "Every time I come into your store I encounter the most unfriendly manager, Shirley, who never seems to have time for even a few minutes of friendly conversation." When her manager shared this comment with Shirley (one-to-one, not with other people around), she started to get angry. But Shirley decided to investigate the situation more fully to understand the customer's point of view. Shirley realized that the time of day when the comment was left was close to the time she arrived at the store. She wondered if this particular shopper always visited the store at that time and was encountering her when she arrived and had a million things to do. Shirley resolved to be more aware of customers when she arrived each day. A few weeks later there was a new comment in the ongoing feedback program: "I want to take back what I said about Shirley a few weeks ago. She was very nice this morning when I talked with her!"

Fight the urge to get defensive! A negative comment is an opportunity to learn and grow. If negative feedback is handled as a positive thing, people will be much more accepting that the comment is valid and might even make a change.

Know what's a meaningful number.

HOW MANY RESPONSES are needed to report useful results? And how far can you drill down into the findings and still have the results mean something?

That depends on how many people, in total, are participating in the program. If the number is modest, you may have no choice but to report on a smaller number of responses. If that's the case, you might consider the findings more "directional" in nature rather than statistically sound data.

Usually a sufficient number of people will participate in a feedback program to consider results valid. Establish a minimum number of 30 responses by category or department as a good rule of thumb for reporting useful results.

Drilling down on the results also requires a sufficient number of responses to provide valid and representative information. But even a small number of responses about a particular issue, especially if they contain specific open-ended comments, can provide insights worthy of consideration.

Share the information.

SOME FEEDBACK PROGRAMS are ongoing in nature. It's easy for employees to forget about them or, even worse, begin to feel they aren't important because the results take so long to come in. To keep the momentum going, management should regularly refer to feedback efforts so employees are encouraged to maintain their enthusiasm throughout the life of the program.

We saw this handled very effectively by a children's toy store chain we worked with. Stan, a district manager, began a staff meeting by recognizing two store-level employees, David and Lynn, whom he had invited to attend the meeting. Customers had complimented David and Lynn's

service in responses given in the company's feed-back program. The two employees were beaming as Stan read aloud the customer comments to every-one at the meeting. Besides offering David and Lynn well-deserved kudos, the other attendees got a very public reminder about the importance of the ongoing survey program at the company.

As results come in from feedback programs, reg-ular communication about the information is a must. Periodically, review the information your company is receiving through the feedback program, even if the program is ongoing. Sharing that information with everyone involved will sustain their interest and keep them motivated.

Deliver *all* the news that's fit to print.

REPORTING POSITIVE RESULTS discovered through your feedback program is easy. Everyone wants to hear how well things are going! But the most important findings include the shortfalls. What is the best way to deliver the results when they are less than glowing?

Prepare people for potential negative findings when your start the program. Make sure everyone understands that a major benefit of a feedback program is learning about the areas that aren't the best they could be. Your program is looking to uncover opportunities for improvement. Before the program launches, clearly communicate this to everyone who will eventually learn the results. When that time comes, no one will be surprised when there are both positive and negative results to review and act on.

And when it's time to report the findings, start with the positive—because everyone likes to hear something good—and then spend a lot more time on the negative results. Most of the value of the program results from making changes to areas that need improvement. Prepare everyone ahead of time to expect *all* the news from the program, good and bad.

Accentuate the positive.

RULE 39 SAYS that the most important results are the negative ones, because they offer real opportunities for improvement. That's true, but . . .

Make sure people are acknowledged publicly for doing things well. Recognize people's strengths, quoting positive comments received in your feedback program.

As you review feedback, be on the lookout for comments about people doing something exceptionally well. When you find these comments, be sure to tell the individual, but more importantly, recognize the positive behavior in an appropriate public setting so that other employees hear about it. By doing this, you help influence the culture in

a positive way. Employees want to know that when they do well, management pays attention. Who doesn't want to work at a company where people's successes are praised?

Another way to effectively use positive feedback is to incorporate examples in training as illustrations of the right way to handle a situation. This can take place informally in staff meetings about customer service or be documented in training materials. One way that companies use customer surveys effectively is to post the positive open-ended comments in the store's break room. All the employees can read them and understand the impact that a particular employee had on a customer's experience. Companies can take this to the next level by recognizing the employee for outstanding work in front of peers and management! Everyone likes to receive this kind of recognition.

Praise employees for a job well done. Share that praise widely and broadly. You'll reinforce company culture, boost individual morale, and provide clear examples for others to follow.

See clearly with a dashboard.

YOUR COMPANY HAS spent considerable time and money to conduct a feedback program. Now the most important consideration is making sure the people who need to know the findings actually read them. This means they must be easy to use. If it is too difficult to access the results, those who most need to hear the feedback won't.

Make it simple to understand with a dashboard. This tool is a website landing page that visually illustrates the data using charts, widgets, and tables. A dashboard makes it easy to see key information in real time and drill down to learn more about specific findings. A dashboard makes it easy for users to find all the information they need about the feedback program in one place.

When we work with a client to build a dashboard,

we ask a number of questions to find out what is most important to the client for utilizing the feedback. From there, we determine the best way to portray that data in the dashboard using appropriate graphical tools.

The alternative to a dashboard is to create reports on the data. This requires more manual labor and usually takes longer to report on the data. An organized system to find reports also needs to be implemented, such as in network folders.

Accessing data and reports from feedback programs should be as easy as possible. A dashboard is easy for everyone to understand and helps to make sure that the voice of the customer or employee is heard.

Analyze the comments.

IT'S GREAT TO have the results of a feedback program show on a reporting dashboard—an easy-to-use visual presentation of key findings (see Rule 41). But a dashboard goes only so far. It illustrates numerical findings and ratings, but leaves out the richness of open-ended comments that respondents also provide. Be sure to analyze the data *and* the comments!

Open-ended feedback provides a great deal of value, adding depth and clarity beyond the numbers. Survey comments can be analyzed to understand trends and themes. You can search for key words used in comments to find areas of interest.

Many feedback programs use a web-based survey. Some include an interactive voice response (IVR) option for respondents to give comments via the telephone, which allows you to hear the real "voice of the customer." These voice comments should be shared with the appropriate individuals within the organization. Much more than the numbers, these comments can really drive the point home.

If you have found yourself on the receiving end of a poor customer service experience, you'll recall the high level of emotion involved in the conversation. We send clients a monthly report of comments received in their feedback programs to provide a flavor of the deeper sentiment behind the numbers. Comments can be positive, such as: "I have a deli guy that I like, and he was there, pleasant as always." "I was looking for an item (in the wrong place) and an employee asked me if he could help me. He told me which aisle the item was located and offered to show me. That was thoughtful." "My favorite cashier was there and I waited in line for her just because she's so nice."

Other times, comments might be more pointed: "On a previous visit I had purchased two packages of eye of round tenderized steak. We have been very pleased with this product for quite some time. When I fixed the steak this time it was not tender but very chewy and gristly. Told the service department and he told me to tell the meat department. She was very nice but did not offer a refund. I had the package info and my receipt. Was a little disappointed."

Whether positive or negative, such comments

play an important role in understanding what is going on at the store level. They get to the sentiment behind the transaction, something you just can't understand from numbers and ratings alone.

Take advantage of the rich feedback found in open-ended comments. And be sure to share those comments with others when the need to convey the depth and emotion of feedback would help them understand more clearly.

Assess, don't obsess.

IMMEDIATE FEEDBACK AND reporting offered by automated survey systems can be a blessing and a curse.

Real-time reporting lets you take action immediately on customer comments. In today's connected world of social media and electronic communication, consumers have come to expect a swift and appropriate response to their input. We encourage our clients to regularly monitor their inbound customer comments so they can react quickly. You can give a sincere and relevant response to the customer, correct a problem that has been brought to light, or praise an employee for providing superior service.

But . . . don't miss the forest while looking at the trees. Automated feedback systems also collect ratings and tabulate numerical data in real time. These numbers can be a distraction for employees and management who deal with customers daily. Numerical ratings and data are best viewed on a longer time horizon—monthly or quarterly.

We worked with a retail banking company whose branch managers would contact us nearly every day about their survey scores. They would ask how their teller friendliness ratings could have dipped two points from the previous day. We tried to help them understand that the day-to-day scores were not necessarily indicative of the whole picture, but they were feeling pressure from their regional management group to respond. We told them not to obsess over each score, and then counseled management to take the longer view of the feedback.

Don't be overwhelmed by every number that comes in every day. Automated survey systems enable real-time processing and reporting of customer feedback, but you'll always see the small ups and downs that go along with individual responses. Match your reaction to the timeframe being reviewed.

RULE

44

Don't complain about complaints.

SUCCESSFUL ORGANIZATIONS CAPITALIZE on complaints to take their operation to the next level. You may not enjoy hearing customers tell you what went wrong, but those complaints are usually the most valuable feedback you can get.

Complaints may surface from a variety of issues—poor service, lack of consistency, quality issues, inadequate training, and more. A complaint illustrates a clear shortfall. A consistent pattern of complaints in a particular area demonstrates a need for a closer look, with an eye toward making improvements.

One of our clients installed a special cooling fan to help keep refrigerated products at the proper temperature. But due to the increased noise from the new, more powerful fan, customers were staying away from the area for fear that the fan was malfunctioning. After several customers complained about the fan noise, the storeowner easily resolved the issue by posting a sign to assure customers that everything was functioning properly.

Treating complaints as a positive helps turn what could be a negative into a chance to fix something that is broken or improve a mediocre situation.

Keep it professional.

WHEN FEEDBACK COMES in and there are negative findings, it is tempting to find fault. Don't.

Put the focus squarely on the results, not on the person or team responsible for the negative issues. Making the results someone's fault will not lead to improved performance.

But remember: while it is not appropriate to blame someone (or a group) for the negative feedback, it is important to hold that party accountable. This means helping the responsible party develop action plans to improve the results and setting regular checkpoints to gauge progress.

There's a fine line between assessing blame (personal) and assigning responsibility (professional). Keep it professional, not personal, to foster the right atmosphere to make improvements.

Paint a picture.

A PICTURE IS worth a thousand words—or more—in a feedback program. A compelling visual clearly communicates a complex idea or data set.

In a large program, there could be tens of thousands of ratings. While these ratings roll up into average scores, the results become much more digestible and interesting when they are displayed visually. There are many different tools you can use to display data: infographics, charts, tables, dashboards, and more. The visual approach is even more useful when comparing results across units, departments, or against the overall organization.

Turn your survey results into pictures to illustrate key findings. You'll make the results much easier to understand.

Use baselines and benchmarks.

THE FIRST TIME you conduct a survey or launch a feedback program you establish a baseline. That's the starting point in your journey to compare against future points in time to measure progress.

When you conduct your first survey, you determine your performance on key measures. This baseline is what you use to measure the results from the next survey you conduct. Use the baseline to set specific targets for improvement.

You can use external benchmarks, too, to prioritize your survey results. Compare your results against industry norms or best practices. Each year we conduct a national study that measures the way shoppers rate supermarket performance on a number of attributes. We compare our clients' results from their own surveys against these regional and national benchmarks to show them how they stack up against the competition.

While survey content can be developed over time, a core set of questions used each survey period provides valid comparisons against established baselines or benchmarks.

Using baselines or benchmarks to set priorities and goals help you know if your efforts are paying off.

Watch the trend.

SCORES COLLECTED THROUGH a feedback program represent findings at a point in time. The collection of scores for a given item or a location over time creates a trend line that illustrates improvement or decline.

If we just examined a single score from a feedback program at one point in time, we might know whether that is a "good" or "bad" number based on the scale used. However, we wouldn't be able to tell if we were making progress towards a goal or if the score was just an anomaly. Feedback program results, when charted over time, show us whether or not we are moving in the right direction.

Many times a store may have an immediate reaction to a score on a survey that isn't as good as desired. Look at that score relative to several previous scores over a given time period to determine whether the trend line shows improvement or action needs to be taken.

Watching the trends helps provide clear insight on the direction of important scores. Trends in the data let you know if you are on target, if a course correction is needed, or if a result is simply an outlier.

Do something about it.

IF YOU'RE NOT going to make any changes based on what you learn, don't waste your time and money getting the feedback.

Some employees at a mail order company were having a conversation on their lunch break. "Did anyone do the employee survey yet?" asked one recently hired employee. "No," said a more tenured employee. "After last year's survey they told us we had a problem with communication in my department. But nothing has changed."

It's a big mistake for an organization to conduct surveys to measure things and then not act on any of the information. If your organization is not prepared to make any changes based on the results of a survey, reconsider. You'll do more harm than good.

Completing a survey takes time and effort, and respondents justifiably assume that their feedback will be heard and carefully considered. It's frustrating to a customer to provide candid and perhaps detailed feedback about a company or an experience, and then see nothing change as a result. And employees, who are often skeptical of their company's motives, will only become disillusioned if nothing is done to address the opportunities for improvement.

When stakeholders understand that a survey or feedback program is part of an ongoing process to improve their environment or experience, you foster a culture that attracts and retains the best employees and customers.

Provide the tools for action.

YOU'VE COMPLETED YOUR survey, you have all the feedback, and now you're ready to take action on what you've learned. Great! Let's do it right.

One effective tool for helping people decide what needs to be done with the feedback is the action planning workbook. They give unit and department managers a consistent format for developing plans to address the key opportunities uncovered by the feedback program. Provide these when the results are communicated within the organization. With an action planning workbook, everyone knows the process for taking steps to act on what was learned in the survey.

Another best practice in customer survey reporting is to provide a knowledge management module, which is an interactive database of concrete tips and useful resources provided by supervisors or co-workers that prescribes specific actions to address areas needing improvement.

One company we've worked with rewards its store managers for the successful execution of their action plans rather than for the results of the survey itself. We think this approach is really forward thinking. When senior management takes this stance, the organization is equipped to truly respond to the needs of its stakeholders. The company is less concerned with the results of the survey and more interested in taking action to improve the operations.

Providing the appropriate tools and actively responding to findings ensures a successful survey initiative.

Show what you've done.

ONCE YOU HAVE reviewed the results of the feedback and taken concrete action, communicate what action has been taken. Let people know what you've done as a result of feedback received, and you'll build credibility and goodwill.

How do you communicate? It depends on the audience that provided the feedback. If it was a customer, it could be as simple as a personal note or call telling them you heard their concern or comment and letting them know what you did as a result of their input. If major changes were made in your organization as a result of feedback, use your website, advertising vehicles, or newsletters to tell your customers about the improvements. For employee surveys, communicate what was done in response to the feedback by articles in the internal newsletter, announcements at company

meetings, information on posters, or other vehicles to reach as many employees as possible.

You can also share what you've done with others who may be influenced positively by the fact that your organization listens to feedback and acts on it. This may include groups as diverse as industry peers, customers of competitors, or donors of other non-profit organizations.

If no one knows you made changes as a result of their input, you fail to capitalize on the opportunity to deepen your relationship. Make sure to show what you've done with the feedback you've received.

Make the next program better.

COLLECTING FEEDBACK SHOULD be considered a journey, not a destination. There will always be ways to improve or refine the feedback process. Start by making notes for next time.

If the feedback program operates as an ongoing survey, new ideas can be incorporated in real time. Review your feedback quarterly and think about which questions may have run their course versus others that remain important. Is there a new issue in your industry or in your organization that is now relevant? Add a question about that.

If your feedback program is a one-shot, such as an annual employee survey, you have the opportunity to assess what went well and what could be improved at the end of the process each year. While the information is still fresh in everyone's minds, it's a good time to refresh your survey questions for next year.

The quality of your information will be best when you keep improving your feedback program.